WHAT · DO · WE · KNOW
ABOUT THE
TUDORS · AND
STUARTS · ?

RICHARD TAMES

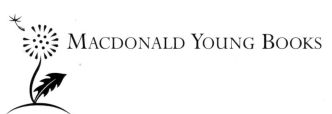

MACDONALD YOUNG BOOKS

Macdonald Young Books
61 Western Road
Hove
East Sussex
BN3 1JD

First published in 1994 by
Simon and Schuster Young Books
Reprinted in 1996 by
Macdonald Young Books

Designer and illustrator: Celia Hart
Commissioning editor: Debbie Fox
Copy editor: Jayne Booth
Picture research: Valerie Mulcahy
Series design: David West
           Children's Book Design

Photograph acknowledgements: Front and back cover: by courtesy of the Board
of Trustees of the Victoria & Albert Museum; The Bridgeman Art Library:
p23(b) (Christy's), p26(r) (V&A Museum), p28(l) (Bible Society, London),
p29(b) (British Library), p33(b), p34(l) (V&A Museum); British Library,
p14(b), p25(b), p43(tr); Christ's Hospital, Horsham, p20(r); Devonshire
Collection, Chatsworth, reproduced by permission of the Chatsworth
Settlement Trustees, p37(t); E.T. Archive, endpapers, p8(t) (V&A
Museum), p9, p12(l), p14(t) (Marquess of Bath), p22(b) (V&A Museum),
p24(t) (Museum of London); The Earl of Rosebery/Scottish National
Portrait Gallery, p33(t); English Heritage Photo Library, p18(b), p43(tl);
Mary Evans Picture Library, p29(t), p31; John Freeman, p35(l); reproduced
by kind permission of the Trustees of the Geffrye Museum Trust Ltd, p27(b),
p36(r); Glasgow University Library, p30(t); Hulton Deutsch Collection,
p20(l); reproduced by the permission of the Marquess of Bath, Longleat
House, Warminster, Wiltshire, p18(t); The Museum of the History of
Science, University of Oxford, p38; Museum of London, p15, p21, p37(b);
National Maritime Museum, p40; National Portrait Gallery, London, p17(l),
p26(l), p32, p36(l); The National Trust Photographic Library, p28(r)
(Matthew Antrobus), p35(r); Picturepoint, p27(t) (Museum of London),
p43(b); Plimoth Plantation, Inc., Plymouth, Massachusetts USA (John
Ulven), p41(b); The Science Museum, p23(t), p30(b), p39(t); Richard
Tames, p41(t); Tate Gallery, London, p16; Thomas Photos, Oxford, p39(b);
TRIP, p8(b) (Bob Turner), p19 (R. Styles), p34(r) (J. Watters); by courtesy
of the Board of Trustees of the Victoria & Albert Museum, p12(r), p24(b),
p25(t); Woodmansterne Picture Library, p17(r), p22(t) (Castle Museum,
York).

Printed and bound by: Paramount Printing

A CIP catalogue record for this book
is available from the British Library

ISBN: 0 7500 1450 4

Endpapers: This cushion cover dating from the late
1500s depicts a hunting and hawking scene richly
embroidered in silk and silver thread.

· CONTENTS ·

WHO·WERE·THE·TUDORS·AND·STUARTS?

Tudor and Stuart are the family names of the Kings and Queens who governed Britain between 1485 and 1714. The population of England around 1500 was about two million people and by 1700 around five million. The population of Scotland, Ireland and Wales roughly doubled over the same period, from just over one million to just over two million. Only about ten per cent of the population lived in cities and most of those were in London. By 1700 it had a population of 500,000 and was over ten times bigger than the next most important cities – Norwich, Bristol, Coventry and York.

ARMADA JEWEL

This superb jewel shows a portrait of Elizabeth I. It was made to mark the defeat of the huge Spanish Armada by storms in 1588. Many people took this event as proof that God was protecting Protestant England.

SCOTLAND

St Andrew's flag

Union flag of 1603

IRELAND

ENGLAND

WALES

St George's flag

ORDINARY PEOPLE

The photograph below shows how ordinary people would have looked in Elizabethan times. Ordinary people had little say in the running of the country. They were just told to be obedient to God and their ruler.

THE UNION OF 1603

From the 1530s onwards Wales and England were ruled as one country. Elizabeth I died childless in 1603 and the throne went to King James VI of Scotland.

The Stuarts ruled England and Scotland as separate countries with separate parliaments until 1707. But the Union Jack was flown on royal ships from 1603.

FAITH AND FIRE

This famous woodcut shows two Protestant bishops being burned at Oxford in 1555 because they would not give up their faith. Quarrels over religion led to the execution of both Protestants and Catholics. Most people who could read in the England of Elizabeth I would have seen this picture because the invention of printing made books cheaper. It would probably have made them afraid of wars with Catholic countries like Spain and France.

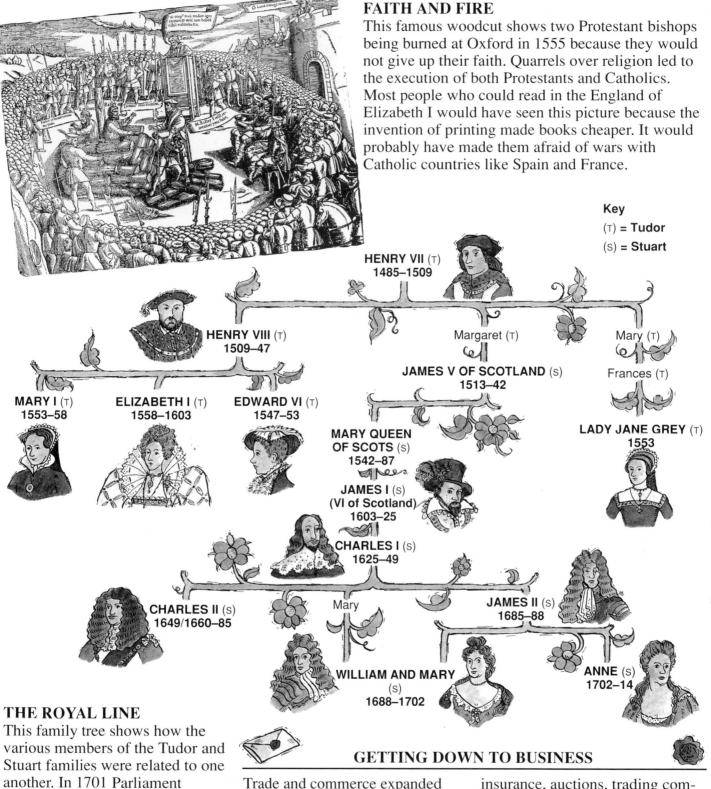

Key
(T) = **Tudor**
(S) = **Stuart**

HENRY VII (T)
1485–1509

HENRY VIII (T)
1509–47

Margaret (T)

Mary (T)

JAMES V OF SCOTLAND (S)
1513–42

Frances (T)

MARY I (T)
1553–58

ELIZABETH I (T)
1558–1603

EDWARD VI (T)
1547–53

MARY QUEEN OF SCOTS (S)
1542–87

LADY JANE GREY (T)
1553

JAMES I (S)
(VI of Scotland)
1603–25

CHARLES I (S)
1625–49

CHARLES II (S)
1649/1660–85

Mary

JAMES II (S)
1685–88

WILLIAM AND MARY (S)
1688–1702

ANNE (S)
1702–14

THE ROYAL LINE

This family tree shows how the various members of the Tudor and Stuart families were related to one another. In 1701 Parliament passed the Act of Settlement which said that it should decide who was to rule. After the death of the last Stuart, Queen Anne, the throne went to a German prince, who became George I.

GETTING DOWN TO BUSINESS

Trade and commerce expanded throughout this period. More people could read and write, which meant more books and letters. Business improved with the introduction of: Royal Mail, insurance, auctions, trading companies and banks, plus (+), minus (-) and equal (=) signs, algebra and decimals, shorthand, sealing wax, envelopes, cheques, printed labels and newspapers.

TIMELINE

	HENRY VII 1485–1509	HENRY VIII 1509–1547	EDWARD VI 1547–1553	MARY 1553–1558	ELIZABETH I 1558–1603	JAMES I 1603–1625	CHARLES I 1625–1649
ENGLAND AND WALES	Strong central government established. **Tudor rose**	Royal dockyards and armouries founded at Deptford and Greenwich. Henry declares himself Head of the Church of England 1534. Bible translated into English 1535. 1536 Dissolution of monasteries begins Union of England and Wales.	Protestants gain control of church. Many grammar schools founded. **Bible**	Roman Catholic faith restored – persecution of Protestants.	Protestant leadership of the church restored – persecution of Catholics. Sir Francis Drake sails round the world 1577–80. 1588 Defeat of the Spanish Armada. Bible translated into Welsh. Theatres established in London.	1605 Gunpowder Plot – a Catholic plot to blow up King and Parliament. Authorised translation of the Bible 1611. Inigo Jones begins building in the Classical style of ancient Greece and Rome.	King and Parliament struggle for supreme power. Civil wars (1642–9) kill 100,000 people. Charles I tried, sentenced to death and executed.
SCOTLAND AND IRELAND	**Cannon**	1513 English crush Scots at battle of Flodden.	1547 English defeat Scots at Pinkie.	**Portcullis on coin**	John Knox leads Protestant movement in Scotland. 1587 Execution of Mary, Queen of Scots. English armies try to conquer Ireland.	James rules England and Scotland as separate kingdoms. Protestants begin to settle in Ulster.	Scottish pledge to resist royal misrule and invade England.
REST OF EUROPE	Renaissance of art in Italy. Spread of printing means cheap books. Muslims expelled from Spain.	Martin Luther begins Protestant reformation. Ottoman Turks conquer Hungary.	England gives up Boulogne to France. Michelangelo becomes chief architect of St Peter's in Rome 1547.	Philip II of Spain (1556–98) rules huge European – American empire from Escorial palace-monastery near Madrid. England gives up Calais, its last territory in France 1558.	Dutch revolt against Spanish rule. France is torn by religious wars.	Thirty Years War (1618–48) ravages Central Europe. **Star-shaped fort**	Royal ministers Richelieu and Mazarin restore power to the Crown in France.
REST OF THE WORLD	Columbus reaches West Indies. Cabot reaches Newfoundland. Guru Nanak founds Sikhism in India. Portuguese reach India.	Magellan sails round the world 1519–22. Mughal dynasty conquers India. Spanish conquer Mexico and Peru. French begin to explore Canada. Portuguese reach Japan. Ivan the Terrible (1544–84) doubles the size of Russian empire.	**Clay pipe** Jesuit missionaries reach South America.	Richard Chancellor voyages to Russia via the Arctic 1553–54.	Turks defeated in sea battle of Lepanto 1571. Tobacco introduced to Europe from America. Akbar (1556–1605) expands Mughal empire in India. Shah Abbas the Great (1587–1629) builds Isfahan as capital of Persia.	Dutch and English begin large-scale trade with Asia. English colonise Virginia and New England in America. French found Quebec in Canada. Romanov dynasty founded in Russia 1613.	Japan isolates itself from other countries 1639–1853. Taj Mahal built 1632–54. Tasman reaches New Zealand 1642. 1644 Ming dynasty replaced by Manchus in China.

THE COMMON-WEALTH 1649–1660	CHARLES II 1660–1685	JAMES II 1685–1688	WILLIAM AND MARY 1688–1702	ANNE 1702–1714
Oliver Cromwell's rule is backed by the 'New Model Army'. Theatres banned. **Oliver Cromwell**	Great Plague 1665. Great Fire of London 1666. *Pardise Lost* (John Milton). *Pilgrim's Progress* (John Bunyan). Tea and coffee-drinking become popular. Royal Observatory established 1675.	Royal efforts to promote Catholics lead to 'Glorious Revolution' and flight of James II to France.	Supreme power of Parliament over Crown confirmed. 1694 Bank of England founded.	Duke of Marlborough wins great victories over the French and their allies. St Paul's Cathedral completed 1710. **St Paul's Cathedral**
Cromwell conquers Ireland.			1690 Protestants defeat Catholics at battle of the Boyne. Irish Catholic majority shut out of government and business.	1707 Act of Union unites England and Scotland. Scottish Parliament abolished.
Frondes revolts of French nobility threaten royal power 1648–53.	Louis XIV (1661–1715) of France – the 'Sun King' – builds Versailles and is the most powerful ruler in Europe. 1683 Turks fail to capture Vienna. **Louis XIV**		Peter the Great (1689–1725) builds up Russia as a great power. 1689–97 War of the League of Augsburg. 1701–13 War of the Spanish succession. 1700–21 Great Northern War.	Britain takes Gibraltar from Spain. 1712 St Petersburg becomes capital of Russia.
1652 Dutch settle in South Africa.	1670 Hudson Bay Company founded to control Canadian fur trade.		Mughal empire in India begins decline after death of Aurangzeb (1658–1707).	

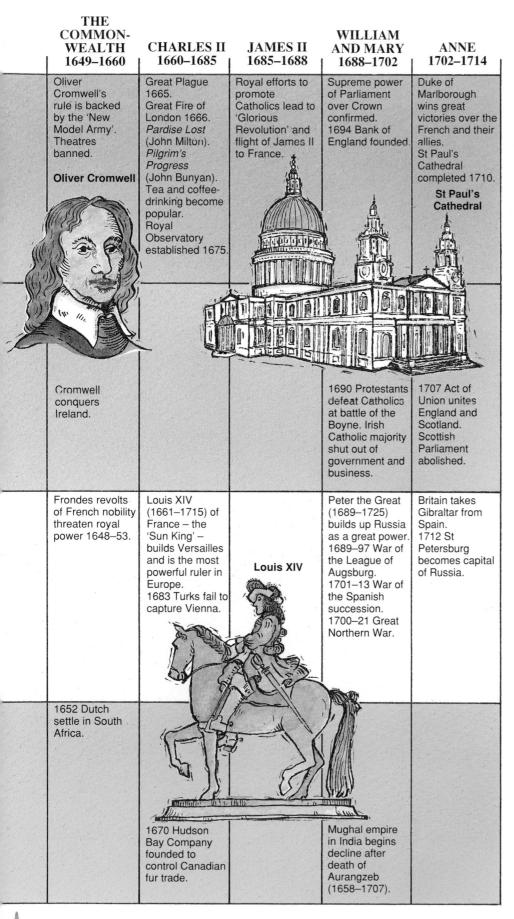

THE POWER OF THE CROWN

This timeline shows events according to the reign in which they occurred. All through this period it mattered very much just who was on the throne. The ruler made all the big decisions about war, politics and religion. Often these decisions were made with the help of advisers – but rulers chose their own advisers and could get rid of them if they wanted to. Royal favour could raise an individual or a whole family to wealth and fame. Royal anger could lead to death and disaster. National fashions in clothes, food, music and building were influenced more by the taste of the royal court than by anything else. Britain was unusual in one respect. Almost everywhere else in Europe rulers became stronger and took less and less notice of courts, councils or parliaments. Only in Britain did Parliament actually get stronger. Charles I tried to rule without Parliament. Parliament tried to rule without a King. In the end ruler and Parliament learned to work together.

A WIDER WORLD

The most important change for Europe, and Britain in particular, was the growth of trade by sea with America, Asia and Africa. The settlement of the French and English in North America marked the beginning of the age of over-seas empires.

WHERE·DID·PEOPLE·GET·THEIR·FOOD?·

More people were employed in growing food than in any other kind of work. Men worked in the fields. Women kept poultry, milked cows and made butter and cheese. Even children could help out with weeding, scaring birds off the crops and feeding chickens. At harvest time craftsmen left their regular work to help gather the crops. Only a few foods, like cheese and salt, which could be kept without spoiling, might be sold far away from where they were produced. Most food was sold at local markets. In 1700, London had 30 markets selling food or livestock.

CHILDREN AT WORK

The tapestry below shows children helping to gather grapes. Vines could be grown in the warm south of England, but most wine was imported from Europe. The men in the background are ploughing the soil to turn it over, then harrowing it to break up the lumps, before finally sowing the seed.

FARMING

The invention of printing led to cheap books on farming, like this one above. Farmers could learn how to grow more and better food by using the best methods. You can see that all the tools and equipment are very simple and could be made on the farm or by the village blacksmith. The most complicated machine was the windmill.

BREWING

People – even children – drank ale because it often contained fewer germs than water. In the 1530s, the German method of using hops to make beer was introduced. Many people brewed their own beer at home or in inns and taverns using simple implements. In Stuart times London had over 20 big breweries. One-seventh of all the money spent in England went on beer!

Funnel

Mash-stick

Mash-stirrer

Brewing implements

FOOD FACTS

Tea, coffee and chocolate became known in Britain after 1650 but only the rich could afford them. At first they were valued as medicines.

Most people refused to eat tomatoes or potatoes because they thought they were poisonous!

Turkeys and geese were marched to London from Norfolk – 200 kilometres away. They were driven through pools of tar and sand so that their feet were protected by temporary 'shoes' on their long journey.

HERBS

Even in towns people grew herbs like rosemary, mint or thyme. These were used to flavour soups and stews and to make medicines, soap and make-up. Saffron was used both in cooking and to dye cloth yellow.

Mint

Thyme

Rosemary

NORTH AMERICA

maize

turkeys

pineapples

chocolate

tomatoes

SOUTH AMERICA

potatoes

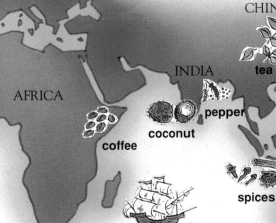

BRITAIN

EUROPE

CANARY ISLANDS

bananas

AFRICA

coffee

CHINA

tea

INDIA

pepper

coconut

spices

INDONESIA

AUSTRALIA

FOOD FROM OTHER COUNTRIES

As European countries began to trade more with America, Asia and Africa, foods from these areas became part of the European diet. Some, like potatoes, could be grown in Europe. But Europe's climate made it impossible to grow tea or many spices, so these had to be brought by ship from where they grew. You can see on the map above where other foods came from. In good weather a ship could sail up to 1,500 kilometres a week. It usually took six weeks to bring sugar from the West Indies and four months to fetch cloves or nutmeg from Indonesia. Can you think why there is no food from Australia?

13

D I D · T H E · P E O P L E · E A T · W E L L ?

The cost of food took up four-fifths of an ordinary family's income. Many servants and labourers were partly paid in food. Poor people were glad to have a cottage-garden to grow vegetables and they kept a pig for pork and bacon. It ate household waste and acorns. Pigeons were also kept for fresh meat in winter. Villages often had common land where people grazed cows and gathered berries or nuts. Poaching rabbits put meat in the pot – but people were fined and whipped if they were caught. Wealthy people sometimes had a bad diet with too much red meat and rich wine and not enough vegetables. This gave them stomach problems or skin complaints.

BANQUETS

This painting of the Cobham family children shows how the rich could afford to eat in around 1550. They are eating fresh fruit at the end of the meal – and feeding their pets! You can see the white cloth and the gold cup. The plates are made of pewter, a mixture of tin and lead.

EVERYDAY MEALS

This poorer family is eating soup or a stew with bread. The father sits on a stool and the youngest children have to stand. There is no cloth on the table. Few people ate breakfast. The main meal was at noon and a lighter supper was eaten in the early evening. Left-overs were often baked in pies. Ale was a regular drink, even for children. Honey, not sugar, was used to sweeten foods.

TABLEWARE

The rich enjoyed using fine tableware made of glass or silver. Decorated wooden 'trenchers', like small plates, were used for serving sticky sweets. As drinking tea and coffee became common, new kinds of tableware like this pot and cup were introduced.

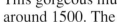
Trencher

Coffee pot

THE PARR POT

This gorgeous mug was made around 1500. The glass came from Venice and the handle and lid were a mixture of silver and gold. It was used at banquets for drinking fine wines brought in from France, Spain or Germany.

Silver cup

RECIPE

Although printing made recipe books more common, they rarely gave exact measures – so cooking meant a lot of guesswork. This is a recipe for stewing sparrows. A pottle is 2 quarts (roughly 2.3 litres). Sippets are little cubes of toasted bread and seething is boiling.

> Take good ale a pottle and set it over the fire to boil, and put in your sparrows and scum the broth, then put therein onions, parsley, thyme, rosemary chopped small, pepper and saffron, with cloves and mace. And make sippets and lay the sparrows upon with the said broth and in the seething put in a piece of sweet butter if need be.

Notice how many herbs and spices are used. Tudor people must have liked things very strongly flavoured. Other Tudor dishes include rabbit with a pudding in its stomach and pike boiled with oranges and ginger.

EATING WELL

On 6 January 1508, to mark the end of the twelve days of Christmas, the Duke of Buckingham gave a feast for 459 people. The menu included swans, heron, larks, peacocks – plus 678 loaves, 259 flagons of ale, 400 eggs, 200 oysters, twelve sheep, ten pigs, two calves, and over 400 other assorted fowl and fish dishes. The total cost was £7 – more than a year's pay for a farm labourer.

In Tudor times up to half the population (about 2,500,000 people) might go hungry if the harvest failed. The last time large numbers of English people starved to death was in the 1620s.

THE SALTONSTALL FAMILY
This painting shows Sir Richard Saltonstall, his two oldest children and his second wife, holding a new baby. In bed is his first wife, who had died six years before. Dead relatives were often painted in family portraits.

When people promised at marriage to stay together 'till death do us part' it meant exactly that. Many wives died in childbirth. Diseases like measles or influenza could be fatal. Even a simple accident, like a bad cut or a broken leg, could kill if it became badly infected. About one child in five died within a year of birth. People thought it was wise to have as many children as possible so that some might survive to look after their parents when they got old. Many children left home when they were ten or twelve to become apprentices and they lived with their master's family while learning a trade. Otherwise children usually lived with their parents until they got married and had a home of their own. Few people lived alone, except beggars and old people with no one to care for them.

The household of the Earl of Northumberland in 1521 consisted of 166 people – family, servants and guests. In 1550, Sir William Petre, one of Elizabeth I's officials, had a staff of 21 at his main home, Ingatestone Hall in Essex. He had another dozen at his London house. The annual wage bill at the Hall was £51 – plus the cost of the servants' uniforms and food. The most important job for the mother of a wealthy family was to make sure the servants were doing their work properly. Servants often got pocket money and tips from visitors. Old servants were looked after even when they couldn't work any more.

A BANQUET SCENE
This is part of a painting which tells the life story of Sir Henry Unton, a soldier and diplomat. His widow had it painted after he died in France in 1596 aged about 40. Sir Henry is the third from the left at the table. Entertaining guests was a big family occasion.

Kite

Windmill

Spinning-top and whip

TOYS AND GAMES
Young children played with simple toys like dolls, marbles, drums, kites, hobby-horses and spinning-tops. Older boys were taught archery or taken hunting while girls were encouraged to do needlework.

BRINGING UP BABY
This high-chair and the two dolls date from the late seventeenth century and would have belonged to a well-off family. The baby who used this chair might have had a solid silver mug, rattle and teething-ring.

DID·PEOPLE ·LIVE·IN· HOUSES ?

Most people built their houses from materials they could find nearby. Where stone was scarce, most homes were built of wooden frames filled in with mud or brick. Near the coast many houses used old ships' timbers as their main beams. The strong rule of the Tudors meant that houses no longer needed thick walls, moats and gate-houses to protect them from attack, except along the border between England and Scotland. Under the Stuarts the first professional architects began to appear – men like Inigo Jones and Christopher Wren. They replaced the master-mason as designers of houses.

BIG HOUSES

This picture shows Longleat in Wiltshire, built 1560–80 for Sir John Thynne, who worked in the Queen's household. It was a very modern design, based on new ideas from Italy. Like other great houses of that time, it has a long gallery where family portraits could be hung and ladies could walk up and down when the weather was bad. Even the homes of the rich were draughty. Stoves were still rare and heating came from open fires of wood or coal. Screens and curtains were used to keep out the cold. You can see the beautiful formal gardens around the house.

INTERIORS

This picture (left) shows the hall of a great house around 1600. Carpet is used to cover the table rather than the floor! There are benches rather than chairs for people to sit on. The walls are panelled with wood to make them attractive and warmer. The only heat comes from the big fireplace. New glass windows made rooms much lighter. Can you see the decorated doorways and ceiling?

YEOMAN'S HOUSE

The homes of yeomen (right) began to have comforts such as glass windows, chimneys, staircases and a tile roof. By 1600 many had separate rooms for sleeping and eating, but servants still often slept on a straw mattress in the kitchen.

FURNITURE

Furniture was usually made by a local joiner. Oak was solid and heavy and would last for many years. Chairs like this one with a padded seat came in around 1650. It was rare to have more than one, which was always for father. Most people sat on stools or benches. Chests were used for storage and to sit on.

Upholstered chair

A POOR FAMILY'S HOVEL

The poor lived in homes that were not much better than sheds. Often there was only one room down-stairs, with a bare earth floor. Sometimes there was a loft above for sleeping in and storing hay, herbs and food. Windows had wooden shutters rather than glass. The thatched roof was a fire hazard – and a home for rats and insects.

NEW THINGS IN THE HOME

First record of carpets in England.	1482
First conservatory built in England.	1562
First piped water supply to private houses.	1582
First water closet (toilet) installed in the home of Sir John Harington at Kelston, Bath.	1589
First greenhouse built at Oxford.	1621
First sash windows installed.	1630
Pendulum clocks introduced from Holland.	1658
First record of a glass-fronted bookcase.	1666
Wallpaper begins to come into use.	1690s

ANIMALS IN THE HOME

Poor people kept livestock indoors in winter to shelter it and keep it safe from theft. Animals also helped to keep the house warm. Most families kept dogs and cats to catch rats and mice.

Hovel

The village priest was supposed to teach local children about religion and how to read and write, but many priests were too lazy to bother. Also poor people often thought it was more important for children to be working than learning. But boys who became craftsmen, shopkeepers, merchants or ships' pilots found it useful to be able to read, write and do arithmetic. Wealthy families often had their children taught at home by a tutor rather than sending them to school. Rich boys were expected to know Latin and a little about the law. Both rich and poor thought educating girls was less important than boys. Girls learned cooking and sewing.

SCHOOL UNIFORM

This is the uniform of a school called Christ's Hospital, founded in an old monastery by Edward VI in 1553. The school still exists and this modern photograph shows that the pupils still wear the same style of uniform.

SCHOOL

This woodcut from about 1580 shows a Tudor grammar school. There were a few hundred grammar schools in market towns by the reign of Elizabeth I. Here, everyone is being taught in the same room. Sometimes older pupils helped by teaching the youngest ones their lessons. As you can see, boys were beaten for not doing their work properly. Almost all the time was spent teaching Latin. This language was understood by educated people all over Europe – at Eton College boys were beaten if they were caught speaking English. Can you see the music on the wall? Singing was a very popular pastime.

Many schoolmasters were under-paid and were often not very well educated themselves. Fortunately the invention of printing meant cheaper books – which helped to give children more information. In London around 1600, about three people out of every four could read and write. But for the country as a whole the figure was only one in three. School hours were very long – from 7 to 11 and 1 to 5 o'clock in the summer and from 8 to 11 and 1 to 4 o'clock in the winter. There were prayers before and after lessons. In some towns rich merchants set up free schools. Other schools had scholarships for very clever boys – but hardly ever for girls. Some let poor pupils in free in return for cleaning the classrooms.

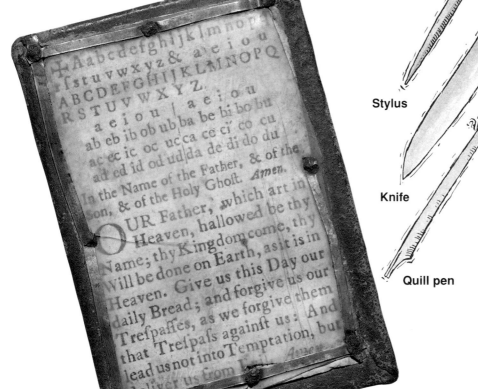

Stylus

Knife

Quill pen

Ink pot

HORNBOOK

The hornbook shown above was made from wood and covered with a thin transparent layer of animal horn to protect the letters and numbers from being rubbed off. Young children of five or six often had one hanging from their waist so they could practise reciting their alphabet.

WRITING

Children practised writing on a slate with chalk. This could be wiped off and used again and again. But writing was normally done with a quill (feather) pen. Clerks carried a sharp knife around with them to keep a good point on the quill. Ink could be made at home, using soot from the chimney. Pencils were invented in Tudor times but were not common until they became much cheaper, around 1800. Tudor people called them 'marking-stones' because masons and carpenters used them to mark out measurements and draw plans. Paper, made from rags, was very expensive. Many more people could scrawl their name than could actually write a whole letter.

Although wealthy people could afford not to work, most landowners were very interested in seeing that their farms were run as well as possible. Before people could work at any skilled trade they usually had to learn it thoroughly by becoming apprentices for seven years. A legal agreement was made between the apprentice's parents and the master-craftsman who was going to teach him. This agreement said how much the parents would pay him to do this and obliged him to feed and teach the boy properly. Girls were rarely apprenticed.

TEXTILES

Making cloth out of wool or linen was the nation's second biggest industry after farming. Four-fifths of the country's exports were wool or cloth. As this museum reconstruction shows, most weavers worked at home rather than in factories. Making a single standard 'broadcloth', 11 metres long by 2 metres wide, provided work for fifteen people for a whole week. Cloth-making areas like the Cotswolds and East Anglia were among the richest parts of the country.

EMBROIDERY

Portraits of wealthy people show that men as well as women liked to wear elaborately embroidered clothes like this glove. Cushions, curtains and book covers were also often embroidered. Rich women did embroidery as a hobby, poor women as a way of working at home without leaving their families.

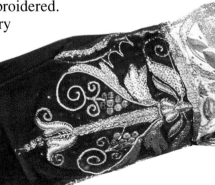

SHIPBUILDING

This picture shows a ship being built for the Royal Navy around 1680. Can you see the holes for the guns? The big naval shipyards employed hundreds of craftsmen. Even so, most worked with hand tools rather than machines. The walls of ships were made with English oak, the masts and spars with pine from Sweden. In 1600, the average cargo ship was about 60 tonnes, and 300 tonnes by 1700.

POTTERY

Potters made jugs and bowls for kitchen use, and large jars for storing and transporting oil, wine and other liquids. Potters also began to imitate the beautiful porcelain imported from China and to decorate their wares in blue and yellow.

CLOCKMAKING

A fine clock like this one would take months to make as each part had to be individually crafted by hand. During the seventeenth century, clocks became much more accurate and were generally made of brass, rather than iron.

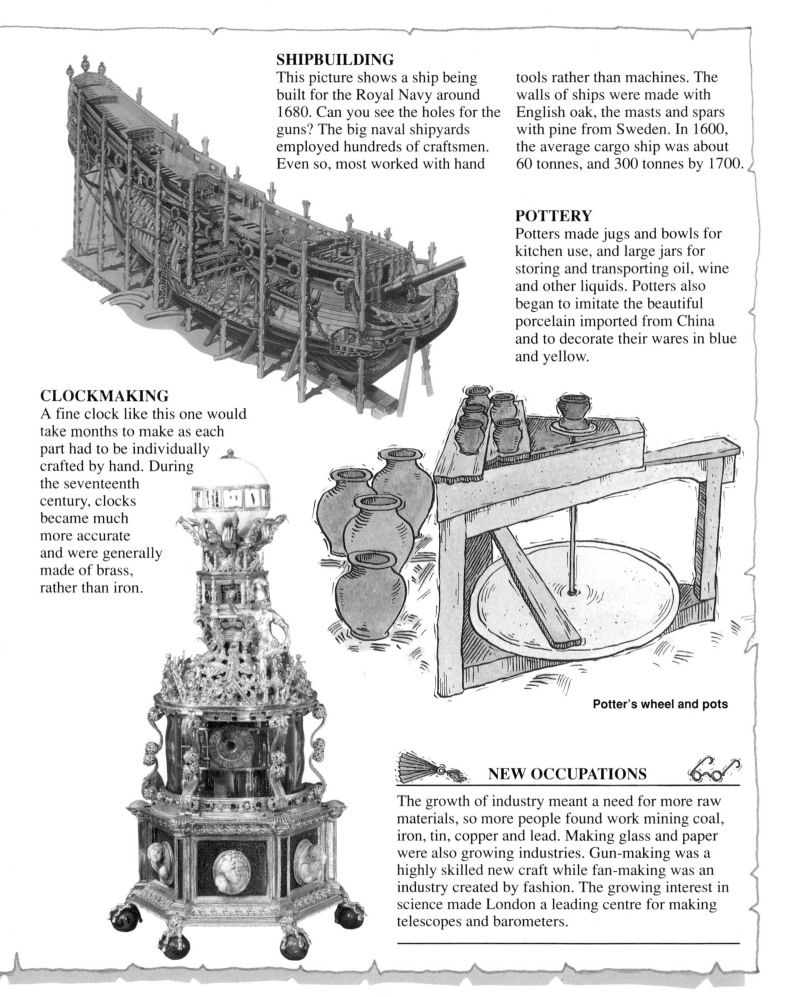

Potter's wheel and pots

NEW OCCUPATIONS

The growth of industry meant a need for more raw materials, so more people found work mining coal, iron, tin, copper and lead. Making glass and paper were also growing industries. Gun-making was a highly skilled new craft while fan-making was an industry created by fashion. The growing interest in science made London a leading centre for making telescopes and barometers.

·WHAT·DID· PEOPLE·DO IN·THEIR ·SPARE· TIME?·

In 1616 the people of Lancashire complained to James I that local Puritans were trying to stop their usual Sunday amusements. The King took the side of the people and gave official permission for dancing, archery, athletics, morris dancing and Maypoles. But he forbade some pastimes on a Sunday, such as bowling and the baiting of bears and bulls. Baiting animals involved chaining them up and setting dogs to attack them. People would bet on how many dogs the animal would kill before it died. James I himself ordered fights between lions and hunting dogs in the zoo at the Tower of London.

FROST FAIR
The River Thames used to flow much more slowly than it does now because it was broader and shallower. This meant that in very cold winters it could freeze solid. In 1564 a fair was held on the ice, with entertainers and side-shows. This picture shows another fair which lasted from December 1683 to February 1684. Charles II visited it with his family.

VIRGINALS
These virginals   a kind of early piano – belonged to Queen Elizabeth I. Her father, Henry VIII, was a talented musician and composer. Singing was a popular pastime for rich and poor alike.

HUNTING

Hunting was important because it gave people exercise, was good training for war and provided meat for the family. This carpet scene (right) shows a horseman with a spear charging a wild boar. Two more hunters have guns for shooting birds. Can you see a man catching a fish? Spears and bows were still used for hunting long after they were given up in battle. Guns took a long time to re-load and scared off other game when fired. Gloves and hoods (below right) were used when hunting with birds of prey.

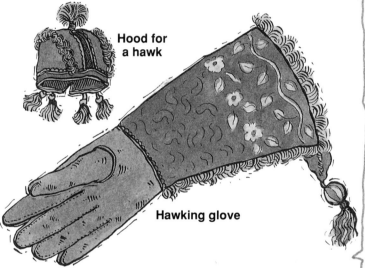

Hood for a hawk

Hawking glove

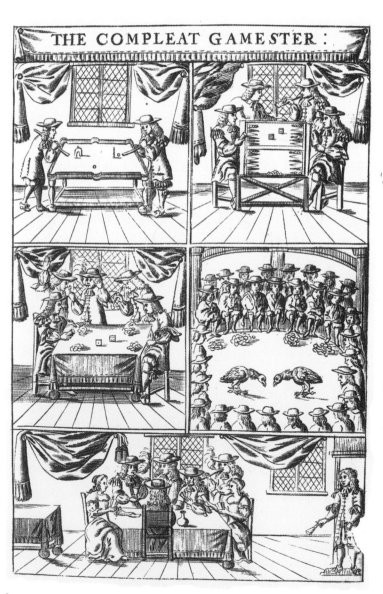

GAMBLING

The cover of this book shows some of the most popular indoor gambling games around 1680 – billiards, backgammon, dice, cards and cock-fighting.

 ## NEW ENTERTAINMENTS

In Holland people skated on frozen canals in winter. Dutch immigrants brought this custom to England and golf to Scotland. Hockey is mentioned in Ireland in 1527. Billiards became popular around 1600. The first organised meeting for horse-racing is recorded at Chester in 1540. Charles II made Newmarket a great centre for horse-racing. Coffee houses also became popular during his reign.

· WHAT · DID · TUDOR · AND · STUART · PEOPLE · WEAR ? ·

The wonderful portraits of Tudor and Stuart times almost always show rich people trying to look their very best, not ordinary people wearing ordinary clothes. Rich people showed their wealth by wearing furs and feathers and expensive cloths, like silk or velvet. Fashionable accessories, like hats or head-dresses, changed every few years. The basic shape of dresses and coats changed every 20 to 30 years. Most people had to stick to simple, hard-wearing garments made of home-produced materials, such as wool, linen and leather. These garments were rarely washed and were worn until they fell apart!

LADY JANE GREY

This portrait shows Lady Jane Grey wearing a dress of cloth-of-silver, lined with ermine, a very expensive fur. The crimson under-skirt is embroidered with gold braid and pearls. You can see how her sleeves have been slashed to show the fine lace shirt she is wearing underneath.

RICHARD SACKVILLE, EARL OF DORSET

This painting of the Earl of Dorset shows the fashion for men of about 1610. Can you see his fine lace collar and cuffs? His breeches are stuffed to make them stand out in contrast to his narrow waist. His armour is included in the picture to show he is a soldier. His head-dress is made of ostrich feathers!

SHOES

These fine kid-leather shoes date from around 1650, when high heels were worn by fashionable men as well as by women. The toes are squared-off and there is braid decoration down the front. They were probably worn indoors. Outdoors, women might wear wooden pattens (platforms) to lift dainty silk or velvet slippers clear of mud and sharp stones. Men wore high leather boots out-doors.

Necklaces

Earrings

Rings

JEWELLERY

Men as well as women wore not only rings but chains and earrings. Belts and hats were decorated with pearls or semi-precious stones. Sir Walter Raleigh paid £30 for a hat-band – enough to buy winter uniforms for seven army officers, plus two pairs of shoes each!

NO FASHION FOR MOST

Most poor people had no more than one or two changes of clothes. This man is selling second-hand clothes in the street. In London many rich people gave cast-offs to their servants, who sold them to make money.

HAIRSTYLES

Hair was rarely washed but often oiled or curled. Ladies also used lace, silk ribbons and fresh flowers to decorate their hair. In the 1660s, long wigs made of horsehair became the fashion for men.

To keep cool underneath them some men actually shaved off their real hair!

· W A S · RELIGION IMPORTANT?

FOUNTAINS ABBEY

In the 1530s Henry VIII decided to take over the lands owned by the church and close down the monasteries. This photograph (right) shows what happened to Fountains Abbey in Yorkshire. Like most monasteries it was wrecked for the wood, lead, glass and stone in its buildings. The end of the monasteries meant they no longer provided schools, hospitals and homes for the old.

Throughout Europe the power of the Roman Catholic church was challenged by Protestants who believed that people should read the Bible for themselves and make up their own minds about what they believed. Cheap, printed Bibles made it possible for more people to do this than ever before. Britain's rulers also tried to control what people believed. Many people, both Catholic and Protestant, were prepared to die rather than give up their beliefs. Others left the country to settle in America where they could worship in their own way. Deep belief in religion went along with a widespread belief in magic and witchcraft.

THE BIBLE IN ENGLISH

By the 1540s, Bibles like this one (left) in English, not Latin, could be found in every English church. The 1611 'King James Bible' later became the standard version.

 BEST SELLERS

The most popular books of this period were all about religion. Foxe's *Book of Martyrs* (1563) is about people who had died for the Protestant faith. Milton's poem *Paradise Lost* (1667) is about the devil. Bunyan's *Pilgrim's Progress* (1678) is about how a Christian can get to heaven.

ROMAN CATHOLICS

The picture below shows the Catholic prayer book and rosary (beads used to count off prayers) carried by Mary, Queen of Scots at her execution in 1587. Because powerful Catholic countries like France and Spain threatened Britain after it became Protestant, Catholics in Britain were banned by law from being MPs, judges or army officers. This lasted until 1829.

Mary, Queen of Scots' rosary and prayer book

WITCH FINDER GENERAL

Between 1644 and 1647 Matthew Hopkins, an Essex lawyer, sent 230 people to their death as witches. Then he, too, was hanged as one. People believed the devil talked to witches through their pet animals.

QUAKERS

The 'Quakers' were founded in the 1640s by George Fox who said true Christians should 'quake' with awe before God. Their proper name is the Society of Friends. Quakers did not believe in priests and allowed anyone to speak at their meetings – including women, as you can see in this picture. Pennsylvania in America was founded as a Quaker colony in 1682.

DID·TUDOR AND·STUART ·PEOPLE· GO·TO·THE ·DOCTOR?·

There were two kinds of doctor – physicians and barber-surgeons. The physicians were well-educated and studied the writings of the Greek doctor Galen, who lived 1,400 years before Tudor times! They knew that diet and rest were very important for curing many illnesses. But practical problems – like setting broken bones and treating battle wounds – were left to barber-surgeons, who cut hair and shaved people as well. A favourite cure for many illnesses was to bleed people by opening a vein or putting leeches on their skin. In villages, poor people went to 'wise women' who could make medicines from herbs or help when babies were being born.

BARBER-SURGEONS

This picture (left) shows a lecture at the Barber-Surgeons' Hall in London in 1581. Many surgeons were very skilled at amputations. Below are some of the implements they used. There were no pain-killers or antiseptics and patients often died from shock or infection. Bleeding to remove infected blood sometimes made people so weak they died.

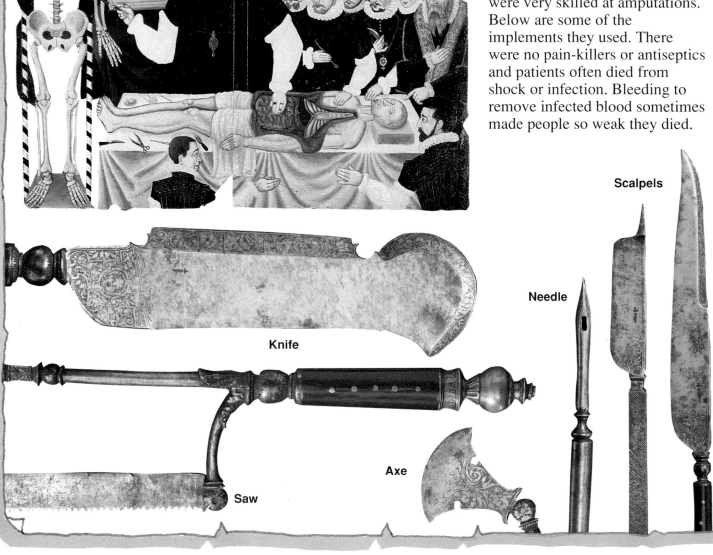

Scalpels

Needle

Knife

Saw

Axe

MOVING OUT OF TOWN

This woodcut (above) shows people running away from an outbreak of plague in a town. Can you see the town gateway? Country people who were terrified of infection often pelted the townspeople with stones. Doctors had no real idea how to deal with major epidemics of diseases like plague. Sufferers were locked up in their houses for 40 days to stop them spreading it to other people.

THE PLAGUE

There were major outbreaks of plague throughout this period. In London alone 20,000 died in 1500, 17,000 in 1563–4, 10,000 in 1593, 38,000 in 1603 and 35,000 in 1625. The Great Plague of 1665 killed 100,000 people. Plague was carried by fleas on rats – but no one realised this was the cause. Smallpox, typhus and measles continued to be killer diseases for centuries.

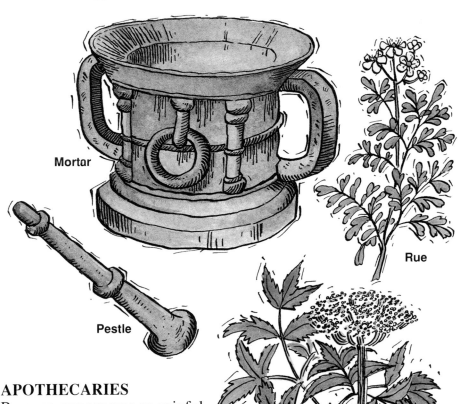

Mortar

Pestle

Rue

Angelica

APOTHECARIES

Because surgery was so painful and dangerous people often preferred to take pills or potions. These were made by apothecaries. The drawing above shows a pestle and mortar. Herbs and other ingredients were put into the mortar and ground into a powder or a paste by using the pestle. The roots and leaves of angelica were boiled with water and drunk by people with breathing problems. Rue, a bitter-tasting herb, was used to improve eyesight. Nowadays pestles and mortars are used by cooks for grinding spices.

WILLIAM HARVEY

William Harvey went to Italy to study medicine. When he returned he became a doctor at St Bartholomew's Hospital in London and physician to James I and Charles I. Harvey made the most important medical discovery of this period – that the heart is a pump which makes blood flow round the body. His book about this discovery was printed in 1628.

WHO·RULED·THE·COUNTRY?

Parliament only met at the request of the monarch – usually when new taxes were needed. Charles I quarrelled with Parliament so much that he tried ruling without it for eleven years. This led to civil war, his execution and the rule of Cromwell, leader of the Parliamentary army. After Cromwell died, Charles I's son was welcomed back to rule as Charles II. He was succeeded by his brother James, who tried to make Britain a Catholic country again. This was so unpopular that his daughter, Mary, and her husband, the Dutch prince, William, were asked by Parliament to take the throne. These events made it clear that rulers and Parliament had to learn to work together.

ELIZABETH I

This portrait of Elizabeth I shows how important it was for a ruler to look rich and powerful. Subjects at home and enemies abroad had to be impressed. Elizabeth ordered that even pub signs had to copy her official portrait which showed her looking young and beautiful!

 ### KINGS AND QUEENS

The Crown Jewels were a symbol of the power of the monarch. The cross on the crown and the orb showed that the monarch ruled as a Christian. Government officials were the ruler's servants and depended on his or her favour. When Henry VIII became King in 1509 he executed his father's unpopular tax-collectors. The personal interests of each ruler dictated how they spent money. Henry VIII lavished money on ships and forts, while Charles I bought paintings. After the execution of Charles I in 1649 the Crown Jewels were sold for £2,000. It cost £22,000 to make a new set for Charles II!

St Edward's Crown

Orb

Sceptre

EXECUTION OF CHARLES I

The civil wars between the followers of King Charles (Cavaliers) and Parliament (Roundheads) lasted from 1642 to 1649 and killed 100,000 people. They ended with the complete defeat of the King. Parliament put him on trial as a traitor for making war on his own people. Charles said he only answered to God for what he did and Parliament had no right to try him. This painting shows his execution in Whitehall on 30 January 1649. It was a bitterly cold day and he wore two shirts in case he shivered and people might think he was afraid. For the next eleven years England was a republic, called 'The Commonwealth'.

COURT OF WARDS

This is a painting of a Court of Wards meeting to decide who is to look after the property of orphaned children until they grow up. Most of the routine work of government was done by committees of men who had trained as lawyers. All over the country, local landowners decided between themselves, with the monarch's approval, who to appoint as Justices of the Peace. Justices of the Peace held courts where criminals were punished, enforced laws about wages and prices, and organised work such as road-mending.

Kings and Queens liked to have their own artists. Henry VIII's official artist was a German, Hans Holbein. As well as painting over 150 portraits he also made over 250 designs for buttons, buckles, book-bindings, costumes and armour. Before the architect Inigo Jones began to plan buildings for James I, he was employed to design scenery and costumes for the song-and-dance masques which James I's Queen and courtiers liked acting (see page 37). During this period almost all the leading painters came from abroad. Rich people employed artists to paint portraits of themselves and their children.

PICTURES LIKE JEWELS

Nicholas Hilliard trained as a jeweller and goldsmith and excelled in painting miniature portraits like the one below. He was Elizabeth I's favourite artist and the first English painter to become famous abroad.

FLATTERING A KING

This fine statue of Charles I stands at Charing Cross and marks the exact centre of London. The King is looking down Whitehall, which is where he was executed. The statue was made of bronze in the 1630s by a French sculptor Hubert Le Sueur. Because Charles was less than five feet tall, painters and sculptors used to show him alone or on a horse rather than standing next to someone – which would show just how short he was.

CARVING LIKE LACE

This wonderful carving (below) is by Grinling Gibbons, an Englishman who grew up in Holland. At first he worked in a shipyard but later Sir Christopher Wren chose him to work on St Paul's Cathedral and Hampton Court Palace. He also did carvings for many churches, colleges and great houses, like Petworth, Sussex, where this carving can still be seen.

THE BANQUETING HOUSE

When the Palace of Whitehall, with over 2,000 rooms, was destroyed by fire in 1698 this was the only part to survive. It was built in 1622 for James I by Inigo Jones. The ceiling was painted in 1635 by the Flemish painter, Sir Peter Paul Rubens. It is meant to show that the Stuarts were ruling Britain wisely and well. Cromwell had Charles I executed just outside this room!

Embroidered purse

Coins

FAMILIAR FACES

Designing coins was an important job for royal artists. For most people a coin was the only way they ever saw their ruler.

ROYAL COLLECTOR

Charles I built up the best art collection outside Italy. He employed both Rubens and his greatest pupil, Van Dyck. The King's art collection outraged the Puritans. They thought it was a huge waste of money. They were also suspicious because many of the paintings were religious scenes painted by Catholic artists or pictures of ancient Greece and Rome showing naked men and women. After Charles I's death much of the collection was sold and is now to be seen in France, Spain and Russia.

DID·PEOPLE GO·TO·THE ·THEATRE?·

The theatre was a Tudor invention. Before then plays had been acted in the streets or in the yards of inns. The actors made a temporary stage of planks on benches and the audience stood in the yard or watched from the upstairs galleries and windows of the inn. Performances were also given in colleges or in the halls of great houses. Having plays indoors meant actors no longer had to shout. People could listen carefully to the words. In Tudor times they would say 'let's go to hear a play' rather than 'let's see a play'. There were half a dozen theatres in London but none elsewhere. Sometimes actors would travel to other towns to put on plays.

ACTORS

In Tudor times all parts were played by men or boys. The leading actors of Shakespeare's day were his friends, James and Richard Burbage, a father and son, and Edmund Alleyne. Only a few actors became rich. Alleyne was so wealthy, he founded Alleyne's School and Dulwich College. Female actresses took to the stage after 1660. Nell Gwynn, a comedienne and favourite of Charles II, was the most famous.

STREET ENTERTAINERS

This engraving shows a street entertainer with a monkey. He seems to be selling bottles of medicine as well. Jugglers and acrobats also used to perform at fairs and markets. At first actors were regarded as no better than beggars.

WILLIAM SHAKESPEARE 1564–1616

Shakespeare was educated well at his local grammar school in Stratford-upon-Avon. When he came to London he worked as an actor and theatre-owner, as well as writing 37 plays. At 47 he was rich enough to live in comfortable retirement in Stratford.

Masques were entertainments put on for the King. They involved dancing, singing and reciting verse rather than acting. The costumes and scenery were gorgeous. In the reign of James I, £2,000 was spent on a single masque – enough to pay for a warship! The famous architect Inigo Jones designed scenery and costumes like this one (right). On public holidays, simpler performances, called pageants, were performed out of doors.

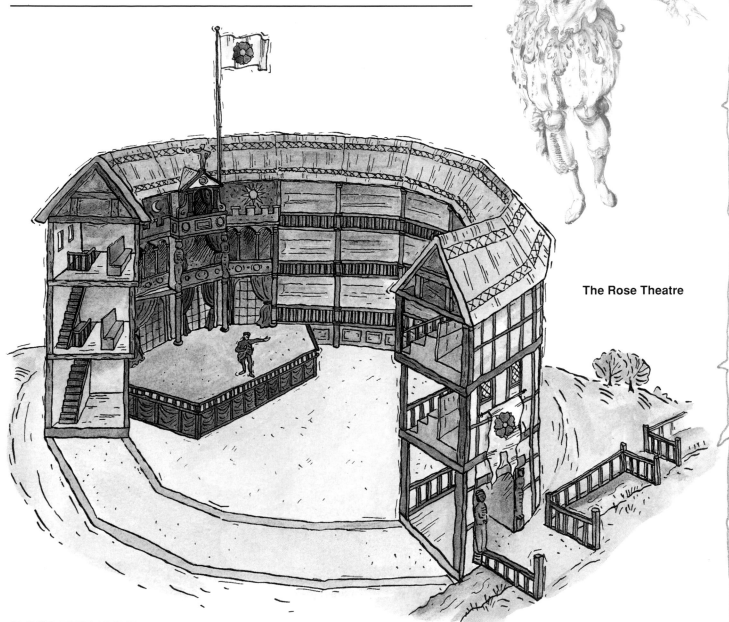

The Rose Theatre

ROSE THEATRE

This is a reconstruction of the Rose Theatre which opened on the south bank of the Thames in 1586–7. It was open to the sky and if it rained the audience standing around the stage got wet. Plays were not put on in winter, when actors toured great houses.

Performances were put on in the afternoon in daylight and so there were no lighting effects. But the theatre was better than an inn yard because there was less noise from the street and some scenery could be used. There were five other theatres near the Rose.

WERE·THERE SCIENTISTS ·IN·TUDOR· AND·STUART · TIMES ? ·

By Tudor times scholars had begun to learn that by making accurate observations of the natural world – from planets to plants – they could understand it better. In the following century, new inventions like the barometer, the thermometer, the telescope and the microscope made it possible to make more accurate measurements and calculations. After 1660 the government began to help scientists by founding the Royal Society, which discussed new ideas and watched experiments, and the Royal Observatory, to improve knowledge of the stars and planets as an aid to navigation. An interest in science became fashionable – even Charles II was a member of the Royal Society. But science had little effect on the lives of ordinary people.

SUNDIAL
This portable sundial belonged to Cardinal Wolsey, Henry VIII's chief minister and the richest man in England. When he used it in the 1520s there were very few portable clocks. Studying the sun, moon and stars – the science of *astronomy* – had practical uses such as telling the time, navigating at sea and working out the calendar. But many people also believed in *astrology* – the idea that future events can be told from the movements of stars and planets – which was only gradually separated from astronomy.

TOMPION CLOCK
The clock in the drawing above was made by Thomas Tompion who made clocks for the Royal Observatory at Greenwich. The clockwork is inside a brass case to keep out dust. This clock tells hours, minutes, seconds and the date as well. Tompion was the first English clockmaker to make small, flat clocks designed for the pocket – watches! He also made clocks that could run for a year without having to be wound up.

TELESCOPE

The first telescopes were invented in Holland and Italy around 1608–9. This telescope was made around 1670 by Sir Isaac Newton, the first man to be knighted for his services to science. He used it to look at the stars. Newton made important discoveries about the nature of light and gravity and the way the planets move through the sky.

This is a list of new inventions and when they were first *recorded* in Britain. They may have *existed* much earlier – especially if they came from abroad. Some – like the submarine and the railway – were not perfected for general use until centuries later.

Bottle corks	1530
Artillery shells	1543
London street map	1559
Firework displays	1572
Guide book	1577
Pencil	1584
Hammock	1597
Signpost	1598
Railway	1605
Vending machine	1615
Dredger	1618
Submarine	1624
Fire engine	1632
Barometer	1648
Air pump	1658
Toothpaste	1660
Yacht	1661
Catamaran	1662
Fountain pen	1663
Slide projector	1663
Fire-hose	1674
Lamp posts	1694
Steam engine	1698

Some existing inventions, like pistols, clocks, globes and spinning wheels, were improved in this period.

Hanc Tabulam invenit & incepit Anton: Verrio, Perfecerunt Gothofredus Kneller & Jac: Thornhill Equites.

SIR CHRISTOPHER WREN

This is a portrait of the famous architect Sir Christopher Wren. He is holding the plans of St Paul's Cathedral which he rebuilt after the Great Fire of London in 1666. He also rebuilt 51 churches and added parts to Kensington Palace and Hampton Court.

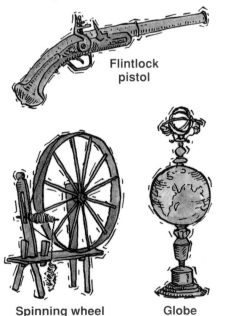

Flintlock pistol

Spinning wheel   Globe

DID·PEOPLE GO·ON·LONG ·JOURNEYS?·

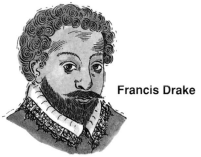

Francis Drake

Between 1500 and 1700, European sailors made great progress in shipbuilding, navigation and map-making. It became possible to trade by sea with Africa, Asia and America. The voyages were long and dangerous. If the winds failed, a ship might drift for days and if there were fierce storms it might sink. Sailors who spent weeks at sea without eating fresh fruit or vegetables could become ill with scurvy. This disease could give you bad sores and make your teeth fall out. But people were willing to take risks on their voyages because they made huge profits from furs, precious metals, spices – and slaves.

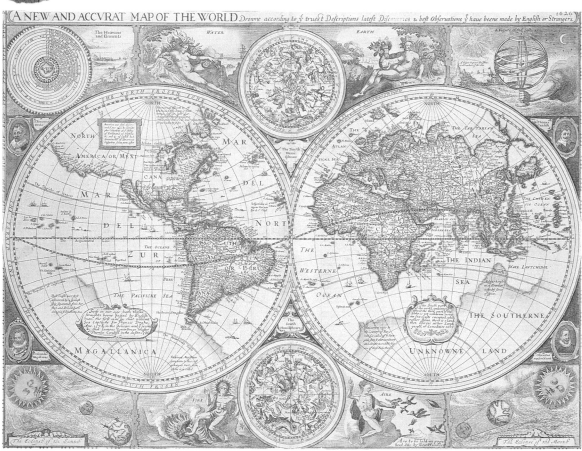

DRAKE'S JOURNEY

The first voyage right round the world was made between 1519 and 1522 by a Spanish ship. No one did it again until Francis Drake, between 1577 and 1580. He attacked Spanish treasure ships and came home a rich man. Elizabeth I knighted him.

This map of the world (above) was made around 1610. If you compare it with a modern map you will see that most of the coastlines of the main continents are roughly accurate. But no one in Europe knew yet that Australia and New Zealand existed.

HARWICH

This engraving shows the Essex port of Harwich which did a lot of trade with Holland. Can you see the star-shaped fort to defend it from attack? Most English shipping sailed around the coasts rather than across oceans. Moving bulky goods like coal, grain or timber was about three times faster by water as by road and was about a tenth of the cost.

THE MAYFLOWER

This is a reconstruction of the *Mayflower* which took the Pilgrim Fathers to settle in Massachusetts in 1620. As it had been used in the wine trade it was a 'sweet' ship – unlike others which stank of fish or animal skins. It was almost twice as big as the *Golden Hind* in which Drake sailed around the world. The *Mayflower* took 66 days to carry its 100 passengers across the Atlantic.

 ## ON THE MOVE

Travel by road was dirty, tiring, slow and dangerous. Coaches were introduced in about 1550 but were not common until after 1650. On a hired horse you could travel about 30 miles a day. A royal messenger with relays of fresh horses could go three times as fast.

WAGONS AND HORSES

Wagoners took goods and people from town to town. The journey from London to Oxford took two days and London to Edinburgh took a week! When Elizabeth I went on a 'progress' round the country it took 400 carts and carriages to carry her baggage and servants!

Wagon and horses

WHAT·WAS ·LIFE·LIKE· IN·THE·ARMY ·AND·NAVY?

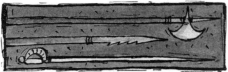

In Tudor times monarchs had a bodyguard of soldiers to protect them and guard their palaces and forts in peace time. But every time there was a war a new army had to be raised from volunteers and mercenaries – soldiers who would fight for anyone who paid them. The navy would also be expanded by taking on fishermen and sailors from trading ships. The civil wars of the 1640s led to the creation of a regular army and navy which were kept going in peace time as well. Guns became more important both on land and at sea. They were not very accurate and had most effect when lots of them were fired off all together. Stone castles, armour and longbows became less important.

Henry VIII

HENRY VIII

Henry VIII was keen to build up both the army and the navy to protect England. He brought over German craftsmen to start an armour factory at Greenwich and he set up a royal shipyard at Deptford.

The Mary Rose

THE MARY ROSE

This battleship was built for Henry VIII. She had 207 guns. In 1545, she sailed out of Portsmouth to fight a French invasion fleet. Overloaded, she capsized and sank. Only 30 of the 500 men on board survived. The wreck was found in 1967 and raised to be put on show in 1982.

WELL FED

Daily rations for a Tudor soldier:
Meat – 32oz   Bread – 24oz   Cheese – 16oz
Butter – 8oz   Beer – 5 pints (Sailors got 8 pints!)

DEAL CASTLE

Henry VIII built a chain of 20 new artillery forts to protect the south-eastern coast from invaders. This one is at Deal in Kent. It is built in the shape of a Tudor rose and has 145 openings for guns to fire in every direction.

MERCENARIES

There was always a war going on somewhere in Europe. Men from poor countries like Scotland often went abroad to fight for a living. The Scots in this picture were in Sweden. Scots also fought for the rulers of France and Russia.

WAR GAMES

This photograph shows members of a club called the Sealed Knot which meets to re-enact battles from the civil wars of the 1640s. Armies then were made up of cavalry, artillery and infantry armed with long pikes, swords and guns. Often three or four times as many soldiers died of disease and wounds than were killed outright by the fighting.

· GLOSSARY ·

AMPUTATION Cutting off a part of the body.

ANTISEPTIC Chemical used to prevent infection.

APPRENTICE Person training to learn a skilled trade or craft.

ARCHITECT Designer of buildings.

ARTILLERY Large guns like cannons.

ASTROLOGY Belief that events can be predicted and are affected by the movement of stars and planets.

ASTRONOMY The science of studying the stars and universe.

CLASSICAL Architecture based on the styles of ancient Greece and Rome.

COMEDIENNE Actress who plays comedy parts.

COURTIER Person who lives as one of the ruler's household.

DIPLOMAT An official sent abroad to make agreements with other countries, usually about war or trade.

EPIDEMIC When lots of people catch a disease at the same time.

ERMINE Type of fur which was very expensive.

HOVEL Poorly made hut where poor people often lived.

HUSBANDRY The art of growing food.

IMMIGRANT Someone who leaves their country to come to live in another one.

KID Type of leather made from the skin of a young goat.

LEECH A blood-sucking type of worm.

LITERATE Able to read and write.

LIVESTOCK Animals bred for food.

MARTYR Someone who dies rather than give up what they believe.

MASQUE Expensively costumed song-and-dance entertainment performed at royal courts.

MORRIS DANCING Type of folk-dancing, originally called 'Moorish' dancing which may have come from Spain.

MASTER-MASON Skilled stone-cutter who managed big building projects.

NAVIGATION Art of finding the way at sea or on land.

ORB Jewelled golden ball used in coronation ceremony as a symbol of the world.

PIKE A very long spear (about 6 metres) which is held rather than thrown.

PORCELAIN A fine and expensive kind of pottery.

POULTRY Birds such as hens, geese and ducks, kept for their eggs and meat.

PROTESTANTISM Type of Christianity based on the right of the individual to make up his own mind about the Bible rather than always accepting what the church says.

PURITAN Extreme kind of Protestant.

REPUBLIC A country not ruled by a monarch.

SASH WINDOW A window that slides up and down rather than opening outwards.

SCURVY Disease caused by lack of vitamin C which often affected sailors because they didn't have fresh fruit and vegetables to eat.

UPHOLSTER A way of making furnishings soft by using cushions, covers and padding.

YEOMAN Independent farmer with a small amount of land.

· I N D E X ·